EQUALITY OF THE SEXES?

EMMA HAUGHTON

The Greek astronomical symbols for the planets
Venus (left), which is used to represent 'female',
and Mars (right), used to represent 'male'.

W
FRANKLIN WATTS
LONDON•SYDNEY

Revised and updated 2004

Franklin Watts
96 Leonard Street,
London EC2A 4XD

Franklin Watts Australia
45–51 Huntley Street
Alexandria
NSW 2015

© Franklin Watts 1997, 2004

Series editor: Rachel Cooke
Editor: Kyla Barber
Designer: Nigel Soper
Millions Design
Picture research: Sarah Moule
Author's acknowledgement:
With thanks to my husband Jon
Rees, truly an equal partner.

A CIP catalogue record for this book
is available from the British Library.

ISBN 0 7496 5348 5

Dewey Classification 305.3

Printed in Malaysia

Photographic credits:
AAP/PA Photos. AKG: pp. 4t (Egyptian Museum, Berlin), 6t (National Gallery, London), 24t (Mozart Museum, Stuttgart), 24b (National Portrait Gallery, London). Associated Press/Topham: p. 11t Bridgeman Art Library: 4b (Christie's, London), 22 (British Museum, London). Corbis/Michael Cole 26b. Emap/Élan: p. 15r. Hulton Getty: pp. 5t, 25b, 25c. Image Bank: pp. 13b, 14b, 28t. Magnum: pp. 9b (Stuart Franklin), 12t (Philip Jones Griffiths), 17l (Richard Kavlar), 21l (Chris Steele-Perkins), 23br (Ian Berry), 23t (Abbas), 29b (Paul Fusco). Panos: pp. 10, 18b. Popperfoto: pp. 6b, 8t, 8b, 12b, 18t. Press Association/Topham: p. 27b. Rex Features: 5br, 5bl, 7b, 7t, 9t, 14l, 15t, 16, 19t, 19b, 20t, 20b, 21r, 23bl, 25t, 27t, 28b, 29t. ZEFA: pp. 13t, 17r, 26t

Quotation credits given from the top of a page, beginning with the left-hand column:
pp. 4/5 1 Proclamation carved on the temple of the 'Holy One' in Egypt; 2 Jane Austen, from *Northanger Abbey*, 1978; 3 'Declaration of Sentiments and Resolutions' of the First Women's Rights Convention in America, 1848
pp. 6/7 1 Christine de Pisan, 15th-century French scholar of Italian descent; 2 Jean-Jacques Rousseau, French philosopher, from *Émile ou Traité de l'Education*, 1762; 3 UK Equal Opportunities Commission
pp. 8/9 1 Polly Toynbee, *Independent* newspaper, 8 November 1995; 2 Charlotte Whitten on becoming mayor of Ottawa; 3 Old English rhyme
pp. 10/11 1 Susan Anthony (1820–1906), one of the first US feminists; 2 300 Group for more UK women MPs; 3 Tessa Jowell, former minister for public health, UK Labour Party
pp. 12/13 1 Martin Luther, the 16th-century German founder of the Protestant movement; 2 Yvette Cooper, *Independent* newspaper, 30 March 1996; 3 Simone de Beauvoir: French feminist, philosopher and author who wrote *The Second Sex* in 1949; 4 Colin Powell, US Secretary of State from his speech made on 7 March 2002, posted at usinfo.state.gov/usa/women, 19:9:03
pp. 14/15 1 Catherine Bennett, *Guardian* newspaper, 20 February 1996; 2 Camille Paglia, US feminist; 3 Anna Coote, *Independent* newspaper, 17 May 1996; 4 Adrienne Burgess, author of *Fatherhood Reclaimed*, 1996; 5 Mary Braid, *Independent* newspaper, 11 April 1995
pp. 16/17 1 Anne Furedi, UK Birth Control Trust; 2 Norma McCorvey who won the right to abortion for millions of US women, but later changed her mind and joined an anti-abortion group; 3 Andrea Dworkin, US anti-porn campaigner

pp. 18/19 1 Rosie Boycott, UK journalist in *The Times* newspaper, 15 February 1995; 2 Demi Moore, US film star, *Woman* magazine; 3 Leanne Cowling, 22, *Independent* newspaper
pp. 20/21 1 Sara Thornton, convicted of killing her husband in 1989 and received a life sentence in jail, she was, however, released on appeal; 2 Helena Kennedy, UK judge; 3 Susan Estrich, author of *Real Rape*, *Time* magazine, 3 June 1991
pp. 22/23 1 Daily prayer of Hebrew males; 2 Rosalind Miles, *The Women's History of the World,* 1989; 3 Buddha, 6th century BC; 4 Mohammed, founder of Islam; 5 Reverend Joan Campbell, the first clergywoman to be chief executive of the National Council of Churches, *Time* magazine, 23 November 1992
pp. 24/25 1 Elizabeth Cady Stanton (1815–1902), pioneering US feminist; 2 French philosopher Jean-Jacques Rousseau, 1758; 3 Pierre Auguste Renoir (1841–1919), French painter; 4 Clara Schumann (1819–1896), leading pianist, married to the composer Robert Schumann
pp. 26/27 1 1996 Cristina Sanchez, who became the first European woman to break into the world of bull fighting, in the *Guardian* newspaper, 28 May 1996; 2 Jim Ballard, the husband of British climber and mother of two young children Alison Hargreaves, in the *Daily Telegraph* newspaper; 3 Elisabeth Darlinson, member of the International Olympic Committee's Working Group for Women in Sport and manager of the Australian pressure group, WomenSport International
pp. 28/29 1 Mary Wollstonecraft (1759–1797) pioneering feminist and writer, author of *Vindication of the Rights of Woman*, 1792; 2 Pat Robertson, founder of the US Christian Coalition; 3 Dolores O'Riordan, The Cranberries, pop group; 4 Helen Wilkinson, *Independent* newspaper, 2 January 1996.

Contents

Changing roses?

Once upon a time, ancient societies across the globe worshipped great mother goddesses. Women in societies like ancient Egypt and Babylon held high office as queens or priestesses, and even the ordinary women beneath them had great domestic and financial independence, often owning their own money and property. In Sparta in ancient Greece, women owned two-thirds of the land.

▶ *Nefertiti, Egyptian queen (reign 1380–1366 BC) was actively involved with the religious reforms imposed by her husband, Pharaoh Akhenaten. She was just one of many queens who had extraordinary power in ancient Egypt. For thousands of years they were worshipped as rulers and goddesses.*

66 *I am what is, what will be, and what has been. No man uncovered my nakedness, and the fruit of my birthing was the sun.* **99** *Proclamation carved on the temple of 'the Holy One' in Egypt*

With the rise of religions like Judaism, Christianity and Islam goddess worship was suppressed and the pagan temples demolished. Since then, women have lived very much in 'a man's world'. The history of this world has usually focused on famous and important men.

66 *Real solemn history I cannot be interested in … the quarrels of popes and kings, with wars or pestilences, in every page; the men all so good for nothing and hardly any women at all.* **99** *Jane Austen, Northanger Abbey, 1798*

From Julius Caesar to Tony Blair, history boasts many well-known male figures. Men acted as the driving forces in society, pushing back the frontiers of science, the arts and business. By comparison, we remember few women: powerful queens, such as Cleopatra, Boadicca or Elizabeth I, the pioneering nurse Florence Nightingale, or the courageous Joan of Arc. Typical female roles as wife, mother and homemaker left little time for exceptional deeds, and

◀ *Joan of Arc (c. 1412–1431) led a series of successful assaults against the English during the Hundred Years' War, and liberated Orléans. But she was later charged with heresy and burnt at the stake. She remains one of France's greatest heroines and became a symbol of French unity and courage.*

women's work, so little changed across the centuries, rarely attracted the attention of historians.

For hundreds of years ordinary women had little control over their lives. Men held power in government, the workplace and the home. But in the 18th century things began to change. Spurred on by the drive towards democracy and equal rights across Europe and the USA, many women began to resent their position in society and started to campaign against it. Feminism was born.

66 *The history of mankind is the history of repeated injuries and usurpations on the part of man toward woman, having in direct object the establishment of an absolute tyranny over her.* **99**
'Declaration of Sentiments and Resolutions' of the First Women's Rights Convention in America, 1848

▼ *Senator Hillary Clinton, wife of former US president Bill Clinton, may have her eyes on the White House, but will she ever emerge from the shadow cast by her husband? Will she be America's first female leader?*

Early feminists concentrated on basic rights such as divorce and the vote, but a century later women and men were still fighting battles across many fronts, including work, politics, marriage, divorce and abortion.

In Western countries women have achieved a great deal, and many people argue that men and women are now on an equal footing. But the United Nations estimates that overall women still do two-thirds of the world's work, earn a tenth of the world's income and own less than one-hundredth of the world's property. For most women across the world, is equality of the sexes anything more than a dream?

▲ *The British suffragettes fought for votes for women early in the 20th century, and their protests often brought them into direct conflict with the law.*

A right to learn?

For centuries girls were taught only how to cook and care for the family, or how to carry out work to provide extra income. This is still true for many girls across South Asia, Africa and the Middle East. Of 100 million children not in primary school, two-thirds are girls. Many are kept at home to do manual labour or housework. Parents often think there is little point educating girls who will spend their lives looking after a family.

66 *Gather what little drops of learning you can, and consider them a great treasure.* **99** *Christine de Pisan, 15th-century French poet*

▲ *In earlier centuries girls from well-off families were taught only the skills they might need as wives and mothers. These often included household management, embroidery and playing the piano.*

◀ *The naturalist Charles Darwin (1809–1882) believed that women were less intelligent than men because of their smaller brains.*

In the past, education for richer Western women often meant learning 'feminine' skills such as playing the piano and singing or needlework. Even Jean-Jacques Rousseau, the French political and educational philosopher who attacked many social injustices, believed women did not need to learn the same things as men.

66 *Women's entire education should be planned in relation to men. To please men, to be useful to them, to win their love and respect, to raise them as children, to care for them as adults, counsel and console them, make their lives sweet and pleasant.* 99 *Jean-Jacques Rousseau, Émile, 1762*

Only in the 20th century has regular schooling for both sexes become widespread. Even so, for many years girls and boys were taught differently, with girls learning domestic science subjects like needlework and cookery, while the boys concentrated on metalwork or carpentry.

Women have smaller brains than men, and in the past this was considered 'proof' that women were less intelligent. Charles Darwin, father of the theory of evolution, spoke of the 'less highly evolved female brain' as 'characteristic of the lower races'. To make matters

▲ *Even today, many of the traditional, top English public schools, such as Eton, still do not admit girls.*

▼ *Girls are now doing better than boys in many subjects at school. Those in single-sex schools do better than those sharing a classroom with boys.*

worse, women's lack of schooling often made them seem stupid. Now we know intelligence has nothing to do with brain size, and girls are proving it. In the UK in 2003, girls scored 8.8 percentage points higher than boys at GCSE and more than 70 per cent of girls got A–C grades at AS/A2 Level, compared with 64 per cent of boys.

66 *We need an education system that enables both boys and girls to fulfil their potential. It's also important to remember that despite the improvement in girls' results in recent years, they are still worse off once they enter the labour market.* 99 *UK Equal Opportunities Commission*

Are girls becoming more intelligent than boys, or is there something about modern life that prevents boys from reaching their full potential? Many teachers say that boys find it more difficult to concentrate and will try hard not to appear 'swotty', while girls don't see studying as bad for their image.

Although girls are doing well in mixed schools, they may do even better on their own. Across the UK and North America, studies still find that in mixed schools the rowdier, more demanding boys gain most of the teachers' attention.

Further up the ladder girls have also gained ground, going on to university and higher education in roughly equal numbers to boys. But few women make it all the way to the top – at Oxford University, for instance, women make up 47 per cent of the students but only 10 per cent of the professors.

Equality in the workplace?

Before the turn of the 19th century and the Industrial Revolution women worked alongside men in many jobs, but as men took up the new factory jobs in increasing numbers, most women were forced to stay at home. Single women who did work were often made to give up their jobs after marrying.

During World War II, however, women took jobs in factories and farms while the men fought. In the US, seven million women worked for the first time during the war – 80 per cent wanted to keep their jobs in peace time, but employment for returning soldiers had to be found. Once again women were told their place was in the home. Even today many people believe working women are taking away jobs from men.

▲ During World War II women worked in factories to produce munitions for the war. But when the war ended so did these women's jobs.

In most Western countries women now have the right to earn as much as men, but in the UK and US they still earn a third less on average. Laws to ensure equal pay for men and women doing the same job often do not work because many women work in jobs such as teaching and nursing where wages tend to be lower. Also, many women interrupt their careers to have a family, and so are less likely to be promoted.

▼ After the war, women's careers were often limited to working as assistants to men.

▶ *Across the world women can now join the armed forces, but in most countries they cannot actually fight on the front line.*

❝ *Young women blithely assume everything will be fine – until they try motherhood for themselves and find it isn't. Having children drastically damages your earning power.* ❞ *Polly Toynbee, Independent newspaper*

But jobs for the boys are gradually disappearing. In the UK, for instance, the number of men and women who work is roughly equal, although many women's jobs are part-time or poorly paid.

But men are now also having to cope with unfair treatment at work – in the US, 15 per cent of sexual harassment charges are brought by men, while the UK Equal Opportunities Commission now receives more complaints from men than women about employers being biased.

So do women have the upper hand? Not at the top, it seems. Women make up nearly 80 per cent of UK clerical workers, but only 3 per cent of company directors.

❝ *Whatever women do they must do twice as well as men to be thought half as good. Luckily this is not difficult.* ❞ *Charlotte Whitten on becoming mayor of Ottawa*

Many women complain of a 'glass ceiling' to promotion. Some blame

▶ *In Western countries women are now represented in most areas of work, and many are reaching positions of power.*

discrimination – women are simply not thought to be as capable as male colleagues, or they don't fit in with the 'boy's club' attitudes of the past. Others argue that women will never be able to play their full role at work until they are relieved of their second job in the home.

❝ *For man's work ends at setting sun, yet woman's work is never done.* ❞ *Old English rhyme*

But most Western women do at least have a choice when it comes to work. In many parts of the world women have to work to support their families, while in Japan and Middle Eastern countries women are actually banned or actively discouraged from working.

In some countries men, too, are gaining choices. Over the last ten years the rising number of 'house-husbands' – men who choose to stay at home to care for their children while their partners go out to work – bears witness to changing attitudes towards the roles of the sexes. What was unthinkable twenty years ago is now becoming common practice in many countries.

Fair representation?

In the early 20th century, women across the world began to protest their lack of political power and influence. Although the British Parliament, for example, had extended the right to vote to all men of adult age, women in the UK were still left without a say in government.

This situation prompted Emmeline Pankhurst to set up the Women's Social and Political Union in 1903 to campaign for votes for women. It stirred up strong feelings for political reform. When a bill to grant women the right to vote was shelved by parliament, hundreds of women protested by smashing windows in government buildings and chaining themselves to railings; many were jailed for their activities. They finally won the vote in 1928.

66 Men, their rights and nothing more: women, their rights and nothing less. 99 Susan Anthony, one of the first US feminists

Women across the world were embarking on a similar struggle. In 1911, Tan Junying founded the Chinese suffragette society, while some Australian women won the vote as early as 1902. The Netherlands followed in 1917, Germany in 1919 and the US in 1920 but Italian and French women had to wait until 1946, and the Swiss until 1971.

▼ *Today in Kuwait women still do not have a say in who governs them, but they are campaigning.*

parliamentary candidates in 1995, in an attempt to redress the balance, but this created a storm of protest from people who saw this 'positive discrimination' as simply discriminating against men.

The vote and political office, however, are not the only routes to power. Women are at the forefront of protest and pressure groups around the world, campaigning against war, hunger and injustice. In South Africa, for instance, women played a central role in the downfall of apartheid. And women were at the forefront of a campaign in India that helped to halt World Bank funding for dams that would have displaced villagers and harmed local endangered species. Is politics naturally a place for men? Or are women hampered from participating in government by prejudice and the responsibility of caring for their families?

▲ Since Margaret Thatcher was Prime Minister in the UK (1979–1990), no women have successfully led a country in the European Union.

Once they had the vote, women began to run for political office. In 1960 Sirimavo Bandaranaike of Sri Lanka became the world's first female prime minister, followed by India's Indira Gandhi in 1966 and Israel's Golda Meir in 1969. But women are still not fairly represented. About 18 per cent of UK MPs are women, compared with 32 per cent in Germany, 45 per cent in Sweden, 12 per cent in France and 14 per cent in the USA. On average women hold just 6 per cent of government seats worldwide.

66 *The characteristics perceived as being necessary to a politician – opinionated, articulate, self-confident, assertive – are deemed suspect in women, who are more likely to be described as strident, brash and bossy if they display them.* 99 *300 Group for more UK women MPs*

66 *Any parliament which is made up of 90 per cent of men cannot be a competent representative body.* 99 *Tessa Jowell, minister for public health (1997–99)*

This inequality prompted the UK Labour Party to introduce all-women shortlists for

▼ In 1999, Helen Clark became New Zealand's second consecutive female prime minister.

A marriage of equals?

Nowadays marriage in the western world is rarely the prison for women that it was so often in previous centuries, when wives were considered the property of their husbands and could be raped, beaten or abandoned without any right to divorce, financial support or access to their children. With many modern marriages now involving joint mortgages and joint

▶ *Marriage in the West is now seen by most as the union of equals on equal terms.*

responsibilities, we seem to have moved a long way since the 16th century when Martin Luther, German founder of the Protestant movement, voiced this opinion of a woman's rightful place:

❝ *A woman is never truly her own master. God formed her body to belong to a man, to have and to rear children.* **❞**

▼ *The idealized image of family life in the 1950s relied heavily on women's work in the home.*

Over recent years attitudes to marriage have changed considerably. Most women no longer agree at the altar to 'love, honour and *obey*' their husbands. Many modern couples now live together and have children without marrying. But for those who do choose wedlock, is a marriage of equals really possible? Studies show that the healthiest people in Western society are single women and married men – marriage, it seems, suits men more than women.

" Men still do not contribute equally to housework, even when their partners are in full-time work. So mothers who go out to work know they will effectively do two jobs, be exhausted and have to pay for childcare. " Yvette Cooper, *Independent newspaper*

Studies in 2001 found that only 10 per cent of Canadian families shared housework equally, even if the wife worked. The wife did most of the housework in 28 per cent of the homes and all of it in 52 per cent of them. News that German men were only doing 20 hours of housework a week to women's 35 hours prompted the German Democratic Party to call for a law requiring men to do their share. Little seems to have changed since French author Simone de Beauvoir wrote *The Second Sex* in 1949:

" Woman is not called upon to build a better world: her domain is fixed and she has only to keep up the never-ending struggle against ... dust, stains, mud and dirt. "

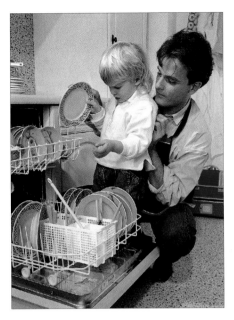

▲ Nowadays, more men are prepared to help with looking after the house and children.

But housework is the least of some women's problems. Although rape in marriage is now illegal in many countries, domestic violence is still widespread. In the US a woman is beaten every 18 minutes, and domestic violence is the main cause of injury among women of childbearing age. Studies in ten countries estimate that 17 to 38 per cent of women have been assaulted by a partner.

" Brutality against women...can never be justified, whatever the circumstances, creed...or culture. " Colin Powell, *US Secretary of State*

But it is not just women who suffer. In 2001, US men were victims of an estimated 103,220 violent crimes by a female partner.

Although research shows women often experience a larger drop in income than men when a marriage ends, many women now exercise their hard-won right to divorce. In the US and UK half of all marriages are now expected to end in divorce; in the UK around 70 per cent are brought about by women. Are husbands responsible for women's dissatisfaction with their marriages? Or are men the victims of feminism, which has stirred many women into demanding more from relationships?

▼ Many women hold down full-time jobs, as well as doing the bulk of household chores.

Babies and beyond?

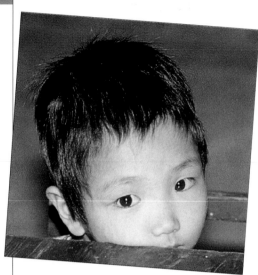

▲ In China thousands of baby girls are abandoned in state orphanages every year.

Being born female can be dangerous. Worldwide, more than a million baby girls are murdered or left to die every year. In pre-Revolutionary China, labouring women often kept a pile of ashes by the bed to suffocate a baby girl; even today thousands of baby girls are left to die in Chinese orphanages, rejected by the parents who want the one child they are allowed to be a boy. In India, women often have abortions if they are carrying a girl, and many newborn girls are killed at birth. Around 50 million Indian girls and women are now 'missing' from the population.

Baby girls in the West usually survive, but childbirth often causes great upheaval for their mothers. Motherhood, many women claim, means always being in the wrong.

❝ Want to have a child? Well don't do it too early. Don't leave it too late. Don't do it before you are nicely settled. Don't have an abortion. Don't have an unwanted child. Don't be a single parent. Don't let your children be reared by strangers. Don't have a child for selfish reasons. Don't be childless for selfish reasons. ❞ *Catherine Bennett, Guardian newspaper*

Despite the increasing numbers of men choosing to become house-husbands, many people still believe that nature designed women, not men, to stay with their children. Yet many women have to work to provide enough income for the family, or to maintain their foothold on the career ladder.

❝ Feminism was always wrong to pretend that women could have it all. It is not male society but mother nature who lays the heaviest burden on women. No father or day-care can ever adequately substitute for a mother's attention. ❞
Camille Paglia, US feminist

Western societies are now also becoming concerned about men's involvement with their families. Increasingly, long working hours are preventing men from seeing their children. A survey of UK fathers found that more than half spend less than five minutes alone with their children on weekdays. This is bad news for both sexes:

▼ Women with young children who return to work need reliable and affordable childcare.

▲ *In the last few years increasing numbers of men have left work or taken career breaks to look after their children.*

❝ *Men are not available to share responsibilities at home and, consequently, women are not available to share opportunities at work with them.* **❞** *Anna Coote, Independent newspaper*

Swedish research shows that men who take time off to be with their children make better, not worse employees – parents in Sweden share a total of fifteen months' paid leave on the birth of a child. But many European countries now give women fourteen months' paid leave, compared to three months' unpaid leave for men. In the UK women are entitled to 26 weeks' paid leave; only in 2003 did British fathers win the right to take 2 weeks' paid leave after the birth of a child.

❝ *Everyone always thinks of mothers and children. No one ever seems to realize that most men want to play just as big a parental role as women, but the odds are stacked up against them.* **❞** *Adrienne Burgess, Fatherhood Reclaimed*

Fathers are now fighting for the right to spend more time with their children, and for greater access to them if the parents' relationship breaks up. It is still the case that when parents divorce or separate, the mother will almost always win custody of her children.

But do women always make better parents than men? Many women think not; indeed many women across Europe and America are turning their backs on their 'biological destiny' and choosing not to become parents at all. British population figures show that one in five women now remains childless – double the rate for their mothers' generation. Rejecting the old goals of marriage and motherhood, many women are opting instead for a good career and personal freedom.

▶ *Motherhood will probably entail a great many sacrifices for this pregnant woman.*

❝ *Motherhood is no longer the only route but a path among many which has its own opportunity costs. Perhaps the fertility rates would always have been lower if men had been expected to take career breaks or forsake their professional aspirations altogether to provide the nation with children.* **❞** *Mary Braid, Independent newspaper*

Sexual freedom?

Before the contraceptive Pill was introduced in 1955, preventing pregnancy was an unreliable affair. But by the 1970s, the Pill and the cap brought effective contraception to 20 million women in the West.

But while many saw the new contraceptives as allowing women care-free sex, others were not so sure. Men began to see contraception as purely a woman's responsibility, while more recently, research has linked Pill-use with a slightly increased risk of breast cancer and blood-clotting. When the male version arrives, will men be prepared to take similar risks?

Just as attitudes to sex have become more liberal, abortion is now more widely available.

Throughout history women have tried to rid themselves of unwanted children by methods such as jumping from great heights or taking poisons like arsenic or lead. Nowadays, in many countries, pregnancies can be safely terminated in hospital.

❝ *The majority has now accepted abortion is a legitimate option for a woman in early pregnancy, where it would be barbaric to force her to continue with the pregnancy and give birth.* **❞** *UK Birth Control Trust*

Although most feminists see the right to choose abortion as a basic right for women, not everyone is in favour. Many women, including feminists, see abortion as the murder of an unborn child:

❝ *I have to take a pro-life position on choice. Women have literally been handed the right to slaughter their own children.* **❞** *Norma McCorvey*

The abortion issue is still being fiercely debated: should termination be condoned only if the health of the mother is at risk, or should the decision be the woman's own, as it is her health, her body and her future that are affected?

▼ *Norma McCorvey (left), who won abortion rights for millions of US women, on a pro-abortion demonstration. She later changed her mind and joined an anti-abortion group.*

Pornography and prostitution are also areas that raise strong feelings. People are divided, often along gender lines, on the question of how pornography should be censored.

66 *Pornography is the theory, rape is the practice.* 99 *Andrea Dworkin, US anti-porn campaigner*

Those against believe pornography encourages men to treat women badly, and leads to violence against women. Others are concerned that attempts to curb pornography are censorship, which can be taken to extremes – a copy of the classic statue of the naked Venus de Milo, for example, was removed from a Missouri shopping mall after complaints that it was 'shocking'.

Prostitution is said to be the world's 'oldest profession', but it also causes fierce debate. Many countries have declared it illegal on the grounds that it is wrong that men should be able to buy sex. But some, like Sweden and the Netherlands, are more accepting, and have adopted laws that can help protect the women involved.

Countries, such as Thailand, have a tourist industry that thrives on the sex trade, with many foreign visitors keen to take advantage of the multitude of establishments selling sex in one form or another. The policies of the Thai government place no restrictions on the age of the men and women involved nor the conditions in which they are required to work. Poverty in the rural areas of

▲ This Las Vegas streetwalker may make more money in one night than many women do in a week. However, while prostitution remains unlawful, she has no legal protection of her rights and welfare.

many countries involved in sex tourism contributes to the plentiful supply of people willing to work in the sex industry because it is one of the few ways that they can earn a living for themselves and help support their families.

But while pornography and prostitution are so widespread, can men ever see women as equal?

The perfect body?

Every society in every age has had clear ideas about female beauty. Sometimes flat breasts are in, sometimes bigger busts are all the rage. In some countries fat is attractive and desirable, in others it is completely taboo.

For centuries women have tried to adapt to these images, often crippling themselves in the process. At the end of the 19th century, there were 100 million Chinese women with bound feet – a process begun at two years old that often broke the toes and forced the toenails to grow into the soles of the feet. Tiny feet were a sign of wealth and status, and essential for girls to find a husband, yet they left women in excruciating pain and often unable to walk.

▼ Fatoumata Dembele, a female judge in the Republic of Mali, Africa. She campaigns against female genital mutilation.

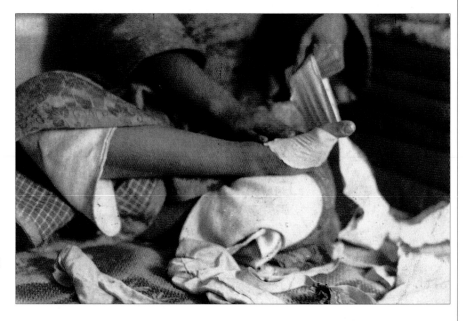

▲ The agonizing Chinese practice of binding young girls' feet. Cloth was wrapped around the foot and toes to stop them from growing, resulting in great deformity and pain.

Today, more than 90 million girls across Africa, Asia and the Middle East have endured the agony of genital mutilation, where the females genitals are cut away and the wound sewn up to ensure that women cannot easily be sexually active. Although modern Western women consider such practices barbaric, many feel they are still judged on their appearance in a way that men are not.

Men do not derive their sense of macho and self-esteem mainly from how they look. It comes from their intelligence and interests. The appalling thing about women is that they still derive their sense of being from the female form. Rosie Boycott, UK journalist

Western women commonly go to great lengths to become thin. Some follow very restrictive diets or risk ill-health from 'crash' dieting (eating very little for a short time). Others put themselves under the surgeon's knife in search of the perfect nose or bigger breasts. From a young age, girls feel under enormous pressure to meet society's standards, shaving legs and armpits, and undergoing painful electrolysis to remove excess facial hair.

Images of impossibly lovely women dominate magazines and television, making even the most glamorous unsure of themselves.

"My eyes are too small and I'm square-shaped. I've no waist and I'm not thin enough." Demi Moore, film star, *Woman magazine*

In the past there has been a great deal of criticism of the super-thin models stalking Europe's catwalks and adorning the pages of top fashion magazines.

"If I see a picture of a model and I like what she's wearing, I feel I have to be that thin to wear it. I stopped eating a couple of years ago, because I was trying to compete. You start to lose weight to keep up." Leanne Cowling, 22, *Independent newspaper*

▲ The British supermodel Jodie Kidd was once heavily criticized for being too thin.
▼ Carl Lewis in a Nike sportswear advert showing that a man can be as glamorous as a woman.

Many people worry that these role models encourage young people to diet unnecessarily, running the risk of developing serious eating disorders such as anorexia or bulimia.

But what about men? Are they simply less vain than women? While a UK survey of 11- and 12-year-olds found that half the girls were already concerned about their bodies, so were a third of boys. In the US a study found that a third of men are dissatisfied with their bodies, and the number of men checking into US cosmetic surgery clinics has risen more than 50 per cent since the late 1980s. In gyms all over the world an alarming number of men are now prepared to take steroid drugs – known to have damaging side-effects – to boost their strength and muscle tone.

Justice for all?

The US Statue of Liberty bears a pair of scales, symbolizing the importance of justice in ensuring equal rights for all. But many people believe that men and women continue to be denied equal treatment under the law.

More women than ever now go to prison. In England and Wales the average number of women in prison rose from 3,350 in 2000 to 4,414 in 2003 – an increase of 32 per cent. Women in Australia make up 7 per cent of the prison population. Women often receive harsher sentences than men, particularly for petty crimes.

▲ *Sara Thornton suffered terrible abuse from her husband before killing him. She was convicted of his murder, but later released on appeal.*

▼ *A women's prison in Bangkok, Thailand. Prison conditions vary widely across the world.*

In Britain 150 women are killed each year by their partners, compared with 20 men, but female killers often receive less sympathy.

Sara Thornton, Kiranjit Alhuwalia and Emma Humphries all received life sentences for murdering their violent partners after suffering mental and physical abuse, yet Thomas Corlett got just three years for killing his wife when she moved the mustard pot to the wrong side of the table, and Joseph McGrail received a suspended sentence for murdering his alcoholic wife.

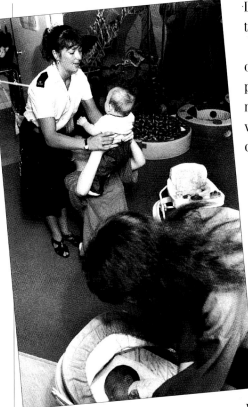

▲ Many women are sent to prison, some for minor crimes. Those with children are only able to see them at special visits.

66 *My husband's violence was very understated. I was made out to be a tart, and a greedy, cold-blooded murderer. I'm really not surprised the jury believed it.* 99 *Sara Thornton, convicted of killing her husband*

There is similar concern about the punishment of rape. US experts estimate that one in four American women is raped in her lifetime, but only one in ten report it and only one in twenty rapists are convicted. In the UK rape convictions fell from 24 per cent in 1985 to just 9 per cent in 1997, even though the number of rapes reported trebled.

Until recently US rape cases had to include an eye witness, while under the Islamic Shar'ia Code of Law a rape victim needs four men to support her account.

While a woman's past behaviour or sexual history is often used to prove she agreed to sex, the jury is not told about the man's past, even when this includes previous rape charges or convictions.

66 *Judges still seem to think that any woman who goes to a man's home is 'asking for it', and so does not deserve the full protection of the law.* 99 *Helena Kennedy, QC*

Most women fail to report sexual assaults because they cannot bear the thought of having to relive the experience in court or face harsh questioning from lawyers. Many countries now try to protect rape victims by allowing them to remain anonymous and forbidding questions about their private lives. But in 1996 a British woman was questioned by her attacker for six days, after he opted to defend himself.

Is the law treating men unfairly too? In many countries men accused of rape are identified, whereas their female accusers remain anonymous. Many people worry that moves to give rape victims more protection in court may encourage false accusations by women bearing a grudge or ashamed of consenting to sex. Others believe men should not be accused of rape if they genuinely believe the woman consented.

66 *In many cases the man thought it was sex, and the woman thought it was rape, and they are both telling the truth.* 99 *Susan Estrich, author of 'Real Rape', Time magazine*

▼ Phoolan Devi became known as a champion of the oppressed in the Uttar Pradesh region of India. As a girl, she suffered rape and abuse, but later emerged as the leader of a group of bandits delivering justice to rape victims and stealing from wealthy, high caste Hindus. She was captured, charged with murder, and imprisoned without a trial. She wrote an autobiography and was the subject of a film — The Bandit Queen. She was murdered in 2001.

God: male or female?

66 *Blessed art Thou, O Lord our God, king of the Universe, that Thou hast not made me a woman.* 99
Daily prayer of Hebrew males

Religious texts such as the Jewish Torah, Christian Bible and Islamic Qur'an have been used for centuries to dictate men's and women's roles in society. Major religions have always assumed that God is male, and that only men can be prophets. They have, therefore, made it seem natural that men should rule women in most aspects of life.

66 *Each in its own way, the five major belief systems of Judaism, Buddhism, Confucianism, Christianity and Islam by their very nature insisted on the inferiority of women…* 99 *Rosalind Miles, The Women's History of the World*

Most religions regard women as 'unwholesome', especially when menstruating or after childbirth. Orthodox Jews, for instance, believe women are unclean for forty days after giving birth to a boy, and eighty days after giving birth to a girl.

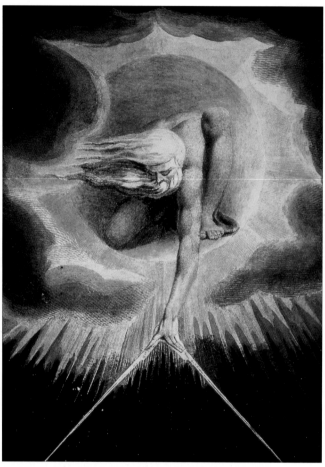

▲ *William Blake's painting, The Ancient of Days, shows a typical image of God as an old man ruling from above in Heaven.*

66 *The body of a woman is filthy, and not a vessel for the law.* 99
Buddha, 6th century BC

Many people believe that religious texts are handed down from God and are timeless, and can, therefore, be applied equally well to today's world as to the period in which they first came into existence. However, others feel that these religious writings reflect the opinions and prejudices of the times in which they were written and would like to see them re-interpreted for a modern age.

66 *Men are in charge of women because Allah has made one to exceed the other.* 99 *Mohammed, founder of Islam*

Religious writings, however, have shaped the way we think about our world for centuries. They still influence the way many women live, from what they can do or wear, to where they can go and the people they can mix with. In countries where Muslim fundamentalism has been adopted, religious rules taken from the Koran strictly control women's lives. A woman must completely cover her body and face or risk accusations of being provocative and ungodly. In Algiers, religious fundamentalists have cut the throats of girls for simply trying to go to school. Other faiths, such as Catholicism, deny women contraception as a means of controlling their fertility.

In the West, however, women are now challenging traditional religious

▲ In many Muslim countries, such as Iran, women have to cover up their faces and bodies in public or face harsh punishments.

▼ The Catholic church believes it is wrong for women to become priests, but many people are campaigning for the right for women to be ordained.

ordained, while the Church of England finally agreed to allow women priests in 1993 after years of pressure by female campaigners.

66 *The fact that God continues to be thought of as a male God means people begin to equate power with maleness.* **99** *Reverend Joan Campbell, the first clergywoman to be chief executive of the National Council of Churches, Time magazine*

Some women believe the language of religious ceremony should be changed to make women feel more included. But many people are opposed to these moves, feeling that existing texts and traditions are the will of God and should not be altered in any way. But if we continue to think of God as male, will women ever achieve equality in modern society?

values, demanding the right to serve as priests alongside men and share in religious power. In the US, Antoinette Brown (1825–1921) became the first woman to be

▼ More women are becoming priests in the UK but they still make up only a small percentage of the total.

Artistic ability?

The world's first novel, *The Tale of Genji*, was written by a Japanese woman in the 11th century, but in general women historically had little opportunity to participate in the arts. They were either burdened with domestic duties or labouring to keep the family afloat financially. Time for creativity was a male luxury:

❝*I seldom have one hour undisturbed. Men can shut themselves up for days with their books. What do they know of the troubles a woman must surmount to produce something half tolerable?* ❞
Elizabeth Cady Stanton (1815–1902), pioneering US feminist

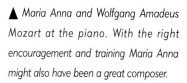

▲ Maria Anna and Wolfgang Amadeus Mozart at the piano. With the right encouragement and training Maria Anna might also have been a great composer.
◀ The novelist George Eliot took a man's name to disguise her identity as a woman and increase her credibility as an author.

The 18th-century French philosopher Jean-Jacques Rousseau spoke for many when he said he believed women should confine themselves to domestic matters and genteel pursuits, such as playing the piano or needlework:

❝*Women, in general, are not lovers of any art, and have no artistic genius. They can succeed in small artistic works which only demand quickness of wit, good taste and, sometimes, the application of reason…* ❞ *Jean-Jacques Rousseau, 1758*

It was also very difficult for most women to get an education, and they were barred from all the top art and music schools. Even when women managed to overcome all these obstacles, their work was usually laughed at, forgotten or ignored.

66 *The woman who is an artist is merely ridiculous.* **99** *Pierre Auguste Renoir, (1841–1919), French painter*

Nanette von Schaden's Piano Concerto in B Flat, for instance, was heard in Britain for the first time in 1996, 211 years after it was written. Faced with such discouragement, it is hardly surprising that even women with great talent doubted their abilities, and often gave up artistic pursuits in favour of married life and motherhood.

66 *A woman must not desire to compose – not one has been able to do it, so why should I be able to?* **99** *Clara Schumann (1819–1896), leading pianist, married to the composer Robert Schumann*

▼ Clara Schumann, one of the great pianists of her day, who thought that composing should be left to men.

Even in 16th-century England, where William Shakespeare was writing plays to be performed for the enjoyment of the masses, a woman would never have taken an acting part – all the roles were played by men. It was several centuries before performing on stage was considered an acceptable career for a woman of good character.

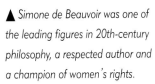

▲ Simone de Beauvoir was one of the leading figures in 20th-century philosophy, a respected author and a champion of women's rights.

Once society had accepted female performers, great stars, from top ballerina Anna Pavlova to film stars like Marilyn Monroe and singers like Madonna, became household names.

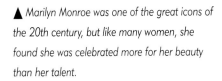

▲ Marilyn Monroe was one of the great icons of the 20th century, but like many women, she found she was celebrated more for her beauty than her talent.

Today many women have successful careers as performers but they have not broken into the worlds of directing or composing in any great numbers. Women in the arts also tend to earn less than men. Even top film stars like Julia Roberts and Halle Berry receive far less per film than their male co-stars.

To encourage greater numbers of female authors, the UK Orange Prize offers £30,000 annually for the best novel by a woman. Many felt it unfair to bar men from entering for the highest prize of any UK literary award. However, the shortlist for the coveted Turner Prize for artists has been criticized in the past for containing no women at all.

Sporting chance?

Freed from the constraints of restrictive clothing and social pressures to remain dainty and inactive, women have participated in sports in ever increasing numbers and are succeeding in every area. In some sports like tennis, women players are as highly regarded as men; US player Billie Jean King helped to popularize women's sport by beating former men's star Bobby Riggs in an exhibition match. More recently Martina Navratilova, Steffi Graf and Serena Williams have joined the handful of women players who have won the Grand Slam, which comprises all the major world tennis titles. They have made the women's game as attractive to audiences as the men's.

Women have made strides in other areas, such as basketball, golf and football. Although they normally fail to attract as much attention as their male counterparts, more fans are following women's sports. In women's football, the 2001 FA Cup Final in Britain drew 14,000 spectators, and the 1999 World Cup had 90,000 spectators and 40 million people watching on television across the world.

▶ *World tennis champion Serena Williams is one in a line of great women tennis players who have attracted today's enormous interest in women's sport.*

▲ *Women soccer players have to work as well as compete in matches; while male players get paid huge sums to play in professional leagues, and can therefore dedicate more time to training.*

When women break into male-dominated sports, they often encounter a lot of opposition from men who feel threatened by the 'invasion'. In 1996 Cristina Sanchez became the first European woman to break into the macho world of bullfighting, amid verbal abuse from male colleagues who believed she should stay in the kitchen.

66 *Bulls are associated with courage, with virility, and some men cannot forgive a woman for holding her own in that environment.* 99 *Cristina Sanchez, Guardian newspaper*

▲ *In May 1996, 24-year-old Cristina Sanchez became the first female bullfighter in Europe.*

Women who participate in dangerous sports face even greater criticism. When British climber and mother of two young children Alison Hargreaves met her death on the Himalayan mountain K2, just weeks after her solo conquest of Everest, people were shocked that she had risked her life. Mothers, they felt, should put their children first. Others attacked this double standard, including Alison's husband:

66 *No one said that the men who died on the mountain shouldn't have climbed it because they were fathers.* 99 *Jim Ballard, Daily Telegraph newspaper*

European and American sportswomen are more fortunate than many. In the 2000 Sydney Olympics, 27 per cent of the participants were women, but 10 competing countries had no women competitors. Most were Muslim nations like Kuwait, Qatar, Saudi Arabia, Oman and Libya. The UK team was 41 per cent female, and the US was 43 per cent. Some governments are now calling on the International Olympic Committee to ban such countries for flouting the Olympic Charter, which forbids discrimination regarding sex.

66 *It is absolutely essential to pursue gender equality in sport, but it is a long-term issue, and the process will be slow and painful.* 99 *Elisabeth Darlinson, member of the International Olympic Committee's Working Group for Women in Sport*

Equal opportunities in sport, as elsewhere, rarely come easily. In the US, for instance, it took a law suit to allow 14-year-old Linda Garcia to play in the New Jersey high school football team, and for 12-year-old Maria Pepe to stay in her local Little League baseball team.

But can women ever hope to equal men in sport? Surely men, usually larger with more muscle than women, will always be stronger and faster? While in most sports women's records trail men's by about 10 per cent, in some, like long-distance swimming and horse riding, women lead. Women might also begin to take part in competitions previously thought to be exclusively for men, as when golfer Annika Sorenstam played in a 2003 PGA event in the USA.

▼ *The climber Alison Hargreaves with her family, shortly before she was killed climbing the mountain K2.*

The way forward?

Despite the achievements of modern science, no one knows exactly why boys and girls behave differently. Some believe the sexes are born with distinct characteristics, others think it is a matter of upbringing. Certainly girls and boys show differences from an early age, but it is impossible to be certain whether those result from their genes or the way their parents have raised them.

But do these differences really matter? Does equality between the sexes mean that men and women should be exactly the same? Since the dawn of feminism 200 years ago, women have argued not that they want to be the same as men, but that they want equal treatment and the freedom to find as much satisfaction in life.

▲ Men may still hold the majority of senior positions at work, but women are catching up and many offices now benefit from a relaxed, mixed environment.

▼ Despite the fact that women living in Muslim countries traditionally lead far more restricted lives than women in other nations, Turkey's former prime minister, Tansu Ciller, is a woman.

" *I do not wish [women] to have power over men; but over themselves.* **"** Mary Wollstonecraft, *Vindication of the Rights of Women, 1792*

But ever since Queen Victoria attacked 'this mad, wicked folly of Women's Rights', the fight for equality between the sexes has aroused suspicion and hostility in women as well as men, that often highlights the true measure of misunderstanding.

" *The feminist agenda is not about equal rights for women. It is about a socialist, anti-family, political movement that encourages women to leave their husbands, kill their children, practise witchcraft, destroy capitalism and become lesbians.* **"** Pat Robertson, *founder of the US Christian Coalition*

▶ *More women now work in traditionally male jobs, while many men are now choosing previously female-dominated careers, such as nursing.*

So has the battle for equality between the sexes been won? Certainly many young Western women now see feminism as irrelevant and out-of-date:

❝ *I don't really get the whole feminist thing. I think the feminists probably need some serious man in their lives.* **❞** *Dolores O'Riordan, The Cranberries*

Moreover, some people now claim it is men who are getting the raw deal. In many Western countries, men are taking second seat to women in education, the job market and the home. In Britain men are evidently at risk – 77 per cent of all drug addicts and 67 per cent of all victims of violent crime are men, and suicide rates among 15- to 24-year-old men have risen 71 per cent in the

last ten years. One survey even linked women's increasing power to higher male sexual impotence.

Others, however, think little has changed. The New Man of the early 1990s, willing to do his fair share around the house and with the kids, seems to have virtually disappeared.

❝ *New Man is being demolished by the culture of the New Lad, the born-again man in search of his fags, football and fornication.* **❞** *Helen Wilkinson, Independent newspaper*

There is no doubt that sexual equality depends on where you live. According to the United Nations sexual equality league table, the best countries for women are Sweden, Norway, Finland and Denmark, which have attacked discrimination with political policies, while the worst include Pakistan, Afghanistan and Bangladesh.

What the best countries show us is that the way forward is to grant freedom and opportunity to men as well as women, giving women more power outside the home, and men more within it. Equality of the sexes means each of us having the courage to abandon the comfort of traditional male and female roles, and grasping the opportunity to do whatever it is we do best. Only then can men and women be considered truly equal.

▼ *Today can young people of both sexes enjoy life together and expect the same opportunities whatever their gender, colour or religion?*

Glossary

ABORTION A medical operation to end a pregnancy, also known as a termination.

A-LEVEL National examinations taken by British 17- to 18-year-olds.

CAP A rubber cap inserted before sex at the top of a woman's vagina to prevent pregnancy.

CONTRACEPTION Methods used by sexually active people to prevent conception and, therefore, pregnancy.

CONVICTION A court's decision that someone has committed a criminal offence.

COSMETIC SURGERY A medical operation to improve your appearance.

DEMOCRACY A political system or society where all adults are given the opportunity to vote and participate in the running of the country.

DISCRIMINATION To treat someone differently for some reason, such as their race or sex. Positive discrimination means giving someone an advantage because of this factor.

DOMESTIC VIOLENCE Violence that takes place within families.

FEMINISM A social movement concerned with women's rights.

FORNICATION Sexual intercourse outside of marriage.

FUNDAMENTALIST Extreme religious movements with strict rules and ideas about people's behaviour.

GCSE National examinations taken by British 16-year-olds.

HERESY Holding an opinion that is contrary to the accepted view or the view of the Church.

INDUSTRIAL REVOLUTION The 18th- and 19th-century movement which introduced machines into many areas of manufacturing, transport and agriculture.

MENSTRUATION The natural loss of blood (often known as a 'period') experienced by women of child-bearing age caused by the monthly cycle of hormones.

PARLIAMENT A body or group that is responsible for governing the country.

PETTY CRIME A less serious crime, such as shop-lifting or avoiding paying fines.

PORNOGRAPHY Material such as magazines or videos which show naked men and women or sexual acts.

PROPHET An inspired teacher or messenger from God, or one who predicts the future.

PROSTITUTE Someone who has sex in exchange for money, usually a woman.

RAPE Forcing someone to have sex against their will.

SEXUAL HARASSMENT Making unwanted sexual remarks or gestures to someone, particularly in the work-place.

SEXUAL IMPOTENCE The inability of some men to have sex.

SHORTLIST A list of people selected for a job, political position or prize.

SUFFRAGETTE A woman who campaigns for votes for women.

SUICIDE The act of killing oneself.

SUSPENDED SENTENCE A punishment without a jail sentence, unless another crime is committed.

TERMINATION See abortion.

UNITED NATIONS A peace-seeking organization of many countries.

Useful addresses

UK

Families Need Fathers
134 Curtain Road
London EC2A 3AR
Tel: 020 7613 5060
www.fnf.org.uk

Equal Opportunities Commission
Arndale House, Arndale Centre
Manchester M4 3EQ
Tel: 0845 601 5901
www.eoc.org.uk

Feminists Against Censorship
BM FAC
London WC1N 3XX
Tel: 020 8552 4405
www.fiawol.demon.co.uk/FAC

Pankhurst Centre
60-62 Nelson Street
Manchester M13 9WP
Tel: 0161 273 5673
www.thepankhurstcentre.org.uk

Rights of Women
52-54 Featherstone Street
London EC1Y 8RT
Tel: 020 7251 6575/6
Advice line: 020 7251 6577
www.rightsofwomen.org.uk

Womens Sports Foundation
305-315 Hithergreen Lane
Lewisham
London SE13 6TJ
Tel: 020 8697 5370
www.wsf.org.uk

Australia

Sydney Men's Network
PO Box 2064
Boronia Park
NSW 2111
Tel: 2 9879 4979
www,gelworks.com.au/mendocum.
nsf/smnhome

International Women's
Development Agency
PO Box 64
Flinders Lane
VIC 8009
Tel: 03 9650 5574
www.auscharity.org/idx.htm

Facts to think about

♦ Of 100 million children not in primary school, two-thirds are girls.
♦ Women make up 80 per cent of the illiterate people in Turkey.
♦ Only an estimated 10 per cent of incidences of domestic violence are reported in the US.
♦ Women now represent 41 per cent of all workers in developed countries, and 34 per cent worldwide.

♦ Men are twice as likely to be victims of crime as women.
♦ More than half the women elected as heads of state or into government have come to power since 1990.
♦ In the US, approximately 700,000 men have cosmetic surgery each year.
♦ In India, five women are burned to death in disputes relating to marriage or property every day.

♦ Women make up 90 per cent of sweatshop labourers, most being between the ages of 15 and 22.
♦ In Thailand, 800,000 girls aged 16 and under are in the sex business.
♦ Of 8,000 babies aborted in a Mumbai (formerly Bombay) clinic during the 1980s, only one was male.
♦ In the UK one in five men earn less than their female partner.

Index